AF254715

THE *Family* WHEEL

D A V I D   F   R   P E R R Y

The Family Wheel

Copyright © 2021 by David F R Perry.

Paperback ISBN: 978-1-63812-119-0
Ebook ISBN: 978-1-63812-120-6

Published by Golden Ink Media Services 01/10/2021

Golden Ink Media Services
(302) 703-7235
support@goldeninkmediaservices@gmail.com

The Willis family wheel is made up of spokes and rims.

Each spoke fits into the rim, and each spoke
in the wheel is a family member.

Each new spoke strengthens 'The Family Wheel'

CHAPTER 1

Tragedy struck the Willis Farm situated five kilometres from Golden Town in outback Queensland. The father of the house passed away leaving his wife and grown-up children, their wives and children to carry on without him.

The Willis family consisted of four boys: John, Mitchell, Peter and Timothy. They all looked like their late father who had been tall, dark and handsome. Their mother still called them all "boys". Each son was a spoke in the large wagon wheel built into the entrance gate.

John was the oldest and with his wife Susanne lived on the Willis Farm, which was more like a commune than a farmhouse.

Mary Willis, a former Scottish beauty and now a widow, looked much older than her age due to the harsh outback conditions. One day she asked John to call the families together as she had something important to say to them

The entire family sat around the large extension table wondering why the meeting had been called. They didn't have to wait long. "Mother Willis" as she was called came in and sat at the head of the table, the place where her husband always sat until his death.

"I can see that you are all very curious, so I'll cut it short. I've decided that I have too many memories here of your father and I feel that I'm getting too old to cope with everything. And I am in a quandary as to what to do.

I wish to remove my spoke from the wheel on the front gate, as I have been offered an apartment in an aged care facility in Rockhampton."

"Rockhampton!" said her eldest son loudly,

"Yes, John, Rockhampton. But unless I have one of you boys and his family commit to keeping our farm going, I'm staying put."

John looked at Susanne, then at his brothers and his children, Michael, Caroline, Craig and young Tommy. They all knew what he was thinking.

"I'll leave you all to think about what I've just said and let you all discuss this. I'll be in my room." Mary was overcome with emotion as she was convinced she had let her late husband and family down.

Susanne noticed her mother in law was becoming emotional and got up, put her arm around her and led her to her bedroom. As she went she turned round to the still startled family and said: "I suggest that each family go to their apartment and discuss this and meet here in two hours to decide what's the best outcome for Mum."

The kitchen was soon empty, Susanne returned and joined John and their children. The look on her husband's face told Susanne precisely what he was thinking. As the eldest Willis boy, it was his responsibility to keep the Willis Farm going. It was a five-generation Willis family tradition.

Michael, the eldest boy, smiled at his Dad and said "My spoke stays". Caroline and Craig agreed. Young Tommy didn't answer.

"If it's okay with your mother, I'll take over her spoke in the wheel," said Susanne. "Thanks. I'll see what my brothers think about it," John replied.

In the other apartments quite the opposite was happening. They realised their older brother John would feel that it was his responsibility and they all wanted to make a life for themselves off the Willis Farm. However, they each came to the same conclusion that, as much as they wanted to, they didn't have enough money to buy houses so they would all have to stay on the farm even though they all dreamed of buying a small farm of their own one day.

Mary Willis had anticipated what was happening in each apartment. For quite some time she had been thinking about leaving the farm and she had decided what to do.

The two hours went very quickly, and Susanne tapped on Mary's door saying: "The boys need to talk with you, Mum." As soon as she read the look on the face of her eldest son and his wife, Mary knew she had read the situation correctly,

"Because you are the eldest boy, John, you speak first." Said Mitchell,

"If you don't mind, I'll speak first," said his mother, "Mitchell, you are correct in saying that your brother should have the first say on the matter at hand, as he is the eldest. And as such, the Willis family tradition states he and his young family should take over the running of the farm if it is their wish to do so."

She stopped, wiped a tear from her eye and, looking at John, continued: "Everyone here, especially me, knows what a great burden running this farm can be in trying times. We have been lucky over the past years that our farm has produced well above expectations. But I must warn you and your family that if you take this giant step, times can get very rough in droughts and floods."

She smiled as she noticed the look of determination on his suntanned face. Knowing his answer, Mary looked at Mitchell, Peter and Timothy smiling, "So, my dear boys, I imagine you have concluded that you are going to stay on the farm with John and his family."

Mitchell looked at Peter and Timothy, and back to his mother. "We don't have a choice, as we don't have enough money saved to buy houses."

"Houses," replied their mother. "You are farmers. Farmers don't live in houses, they live in farmhouses."

With a look on his face of utter confusion, Peter asked "What do you mean Mum?" He knew the only farmhouse on the Willis Farm was their mother's home and John and his family would be moving in there.

"I've known for some time that while you have spent your entire lives working on this farm, you have all dreamt of one day owning your own farms." Mary noticed that her sons had no idea what she was talking about,

"John, as the eldest boy in the Willis family, I am giving you first choice. You or one of your brothers can take over the ownership of the Willis Farm from me, or I'm putting it up for sale. I would like it to continue as would your father. So I've decided to offer you first choice, John -- the Willis Farm or $400,000."

Mary opened a wallet she was holding and said, "I'm holding four bank cheques for $400,000", and handed one each to her boys, as she still called them.

"John and Susanne, you have the first choice. The Willis Farm is yours if you tear up the cheque." Without hesitation, John ripped up the cheque and handed it back to his mother who said to him, "Congratulations Farmer John Willis! You are now the sole heir and owner of the Willis Farm. I will have our solicitor write up the papers tomorrow.

"Mitchell, Peter and Timothy, there is enough money to buy a small farm, or you can buy one together. So good luck! I know your father would, if he could, thank you for all the hard work that you boys and John have put in over the years. So please accept this money on behalf of him and myself."

That night the boys celebrated well into the night with their wives. The following morning they deposited the cheques into the bank and each brought a Rural Property Guide. The three brothers decided if their mother was going into an aged care facility at Rockhampton, they should check out crop farms for sale around there. They found they were all too expensive and so decided to put their money together and bought a large farm that had three dwellings on it. The three families soon moved onto the new Willis Farm at Rockhampton.

CHAPTER 2

Quite a few years earlier…

When Susanne had just turned 18 she lived with her mum and dad in a little shack in Roma, an outback town in Queensland. Her father worked at the local garage, pumping petrol and repairing broken down vehicles of any kind. She was quite tall and beautiful and her blonde hair and blue eyes made her stand out in any crowd. Since she started to develop at the age of 15, boys were always trying to seduce her, without any luck,

The family had often thought about backpacking around Australia and Suzanne used to think to herself that she would to love to travel around Australia.

When one day she was looking at a map of Australia, she noticed a place called Emerald. "Emerald, what a lovely name for a town. I love emeralds. I wonder if I can find some emeralds there." A few more train stations along the line was a place called Golden Town. "That could be even better," she thought. "I love gold even more than emeralds."

So she started saving money by working with her father at the garage. When she thought she had saved enough, she bought a backpack, kissed her mum and dad goodbye, and hopped on a train to Golden Town.

What she found was a railway station, a hotel, a few shops and a community hall, a tiny bank and a police station and a house with a red cross on it which she thought must be the hospital.

This was not at all what she had expected. Young Susanne expected to find at least a dozen boarding houses. She thought to herself, "I have to find a place to live. I wonder if anyone at the local shops would know where I can find lodgings for a week or two."

Taped to the window of the local grocery store was an advertisement for a "room to let. With the use of everything in the house, including the wireless."

She took the notice off the window and listened to the shop keeper complaining about people sticking things on his clean shop window. After he had finished, she handed him the note saying politely, "Do you know where I can find this place?"

He looked at the sign and took her out to the front of the shop and pointed to a little cottage, next to Golden Town's community hall. "That's it over there, next to the hall. Mrs Greenaway is a bit of a nosey parker but nice enough, I guess. Will you be staying long?"

"Not sure. I liked the name of the town, so I made it my first place to stop as I'm backpacking around Australia. I thought that if I found some gold or possibly emeralds here, I could sell some on the way."

He looked at her smiling, saying, "Sorry to disappoint you. I didn't get your name."

"Susanne, I've lived in Roma all my life."

"Well, Susanne, I have some bad news for you, love. The only mining here in Golden Town is coal mining. And the town that you passed on the train called Emerald isn't named after the emerald jewel, but the green pastures."

Susanne was taken by surprise by this. Her first thought was to head back home to Roma but this only lasted a second. She thanked him and walked up the road to Mrs Greenaway's little cottage and knocked on the door. An old lady with grey hair and glasses, with a blanket over her shoulders, opened the door,

"I believe you have a room that I can use. I'm not sure how long I'll be staying though, as I was just told by the shop keeper across the road that there's no gold here in Golden Town, or even emeralds in Emerald."

"Come in. I'll show you the room. I'm sure you'll like it. It faces north so it's a warm room, which is good in the winter but hot in summer. But I have heavy curtains that block most of the heat."

They walked into the hall. "Here it is. And it's convenient to the bathroom," she said, pointing to a closed-door opposite. "I didn't get your name, sweetie."

"Its Susanne, And I've just travelled from Roma."

They walked in, and Susanne noticed straight away a picture of a man on the wall, with eyes that seemed to follow her.

"That's Fred, my late husband; I'll take the picture down if you wish."

"Please."

Susanne settled in. Some time later she was buying a few groceries when she noticed a note on the grocer's front window. It was about a dance in three Saturday nights time in the community hall next door. She had been about to catch a train and move on but she decided to stay another month in Golden Town.

At the dance, she met a young farmer by the name of John Willis. He introduced himself and said to her, "I'm John Willis. You must be the beautiful new girl in town, who came to Golden Town to dig up gold and emeralds, and stayed. You're quite a legend in these parts, you know."

"No, I didn't know. And thanks for telling me! How was I supposed to know there was no gold here or emeralds in Emerald? There's no need to poke fun at me!"

"Sorry Susanne, I wasn't poking fun at you. Its an easy mistake to make. And you're not the first. All the others who were fooled by the names Golden Town and Emerald caught the next train out of here. It doesn't have much going for it, I guess. But you stayed. Why?"

"For this bloody dance! And I obviously should have left like the other idiots who were fooled like me before!"

"Come on, let's dance."

They started dancing. Young man after young man wanted to dance with the beautiful Susanne and this slowly started to get to John Willis who finally broke in and wouldn't let anyone else dance with her.

"You don't own me, you know!" Susan said to the handsome, tanned smiling face looking at her.

"No, but I wished I did!"

Susan noticed that he was genuinely interested in her, and they danced the night away.

"How long do you plan to stay here after this dance?"

"I'm paid up til next Saturday."

"Next Saturday?"

"Yes, why?"

"That doesn't give me much time to persuade you to stay."

"Why would you want me to stay here anyway? We've only just met."

"Because you're the most beautiful girl I've ever met." This made Susanne blush.

That night John and Susanne did not sleep a wink. John was wondering how he could manage to keep her in Golden Town and Susanne was having second thoughts about leaving.

The following afternoon straight after work, John grabbed the farm ute and drove to where Susanne was staying. He was met at the door by Mrs Greenaway who called out to Susanne, "You have a young good looking visitor to see you!"

Susanne thought to herself, 'I hope its farmer John." She quickly checked her hair, straightened her dress and, came out saying, "So what are the locals making fun of me about this time?"

He laughed at her, saying, "Everyone's telling me how beautiful you are, and not to let you go. I didn't sleep at all last night thinking about you, Susanne. So I've decided to see if you'd like to come and have a look at my parent's farm."

"I'd love to. Can I go like this?"

"I was hoping that you'd say yes!"

They spent that afternoon playing with the baby lambs and sheepdogs and meeting his mother and John's three brothers, who all liked her straight away. John's father smiled at her, winked at his son and walked to a shearing shed, waving goodbye.

CHAPTER 3

John and Suzanne often did some shopping at Harry's grocery store. Harry was a happy man who couldn't wait for his next customer to walk in the door. Not so much to sell them things as he knew he had a monopoly, being the only grocer in Golden Town, Harry loved the company and loved to chat with his customers.

He often called Mrs Greenaway across the road a gossip, but compared to Harry, John told Susanne, he was more of a gossip, and the locals called him the Daily Bugle.

He especially liked getting his deliveries, which were brought by a young lady called Veronica. As soon as Veronica's truck was empty, they went inside and a closed sign was hung. The door was locked and the blinds closed.

Everyone thought all sorts of things were happening behind those blinds. The rumours got to Mrs Greenaway who one day watched as the blinds closed, checked no one was coming and then walked nonchalantly across the road. When she got to the front of the shop, she tried unsuccessfully to peek in but couldn't see anything so she went around the back.

Harry heard her outside and held a finger up to his mouth, smiling at Veronica. They quietly walked to the window and grabbed a curtain each. On Harry's signal they opened the curtains. Mrs Greenaway, who had her ear to the window, was startled to see Harry and Veronica standing there fully dressed, laughing at her.

Knowing that she was embarrassed, Harry opened the window and said, "Mrs Greenaway, meet my daughter Veronica. Come to the side door. We were just about to have a cup of tea. Please join us."

Stunned and not knowing what to say, she nodded and said yes.

They sat down and were sipping their tea when Harry said, "I don't see my daughter very often. And I'd heard you'd been spreading rumours about Veronica and me. So now you know the truth. You can tell everyone how we caught you spying on us."

They all burst out laughing, as Mrs Greenaway saw the funny side of what just happened.

"I think I prefer my original suspicion, Harry." This made them all laugh again.

"Mrs Greenaway, please keep what you've found here today a secret. This sleepyhead town needs something exciting to talk about," said Harry laughing.

From that day on, every time Mrs Greenaway bought groceries, she would ask Harry, "How's Veronica?" And they would burst into laughter.

The following Saturday, it was decision time for Susanne who asked Mrs Willis if she could have the room for another month or two. Mrs Greenaway was pleased as she was the perfect tenant, hardly ever there and when she was home was busy cleaning the house.

Susanne managed to get a job at the local grocery store three days a week and found that she loved Golden Town and fell in love with John Willis.

John and Susanne dated, for six months, got married and Susanne moved into the Willis farm.

CHAPTER 4

The Willis farm had a large entrance gate which consisted of a huge wagon wheel and the name: THE WILLIS FARM in bold lettering. Each family member was a spoke in the wheel. John Willis happily worked the farm from sunrise until dusk, seven days a week, and when his children were old enough, they received a spoke and worked on the farm with their farmer.

Unlike her husband, Susanne Willis had light blue eyes and long blonde hair and always wore pastel shades. The two eldest boys had the same colouring as their father, with hazel eyes and dark brown hair. Tommy was blonde like their mother and his sister Caroline.

Susanne was well-educated and had a strong character herself. She gave their children home tuition with the help of the School of the Air. Susanne was filling in with their education while they were waiting for a new governess. When the children were too old for School of the Air, Susanne continued their education for three hours every day after they finished working on the farm.

The youngest in the Willis family, Tommy, was the last of the Willis children still at School of the Air and often rebelled, refusing to do anything, preferring to sit there sulking, saying, "I hate this stupid school work! And I'm not going to do it!"

When Tommy was old enough, he was expected to help on the farm like his brothers and sister. But Tommy did not believe he had to and did not want to improve the farm like his brothers and sister. He wanted to play computer games day and night in his room. Whenever he was asked to help, he always refused and shouted so the others could hear, "I'm Tommy Willis, and I'm not a spoke in anyone's wheel. So there!"

No matter how hard every family member tried to coax him into helping, he steadfastly refused and continued to play computer games. He only joined the rest of the family at tea time and then he went straight back to his computer. Working on the farm was a definite no for Tommy Willis. The Willis family wheel appeared to be holding up without his help so Tommy didn't care.

CHAPTER 5

Craig was different from his brothers and sister, and took after his mother. He was lightly built for a 17 year-old but still managed to do his fair share of the farm work.

One night Craig was sitting in his room reading the family Holy Bible when something made him look out of his window. He watched in amazement as a meteor passed by. He ran outside and watched it disappear into the distance. This sighting had a profound effect on 17 year old Craig. From that moment on, almost every night throughout the year he sat on the porch awaiting another 'Heavenly Sighting', as he called it.

Sometimes family members would join him, but he mostly sat there alone and often fell asleep, only to wake up cold and wander off to bed. After quite some time, Craig could name almost all the stars, planets and constellations. He wondered to himself, 'I know God is up there among those stars. I wonder where?'

His family got used to his unusual ways. His father worried about him being different but kept his thoughts to himself. His mother loved the fact that he was attentive like her, and was passive.

Susanne Willis understood and fiercely protected the individuality of her children. From the eldest Michael, who would fight at the drop of a hat, his sister Caroline's feisty nature, the youngest Tommy's stubbornness, to Craig who wouldn't hurt a fly, she loved the fact that they were all very different.

Caroline, who was an 18 year old tall, blonde, blue-eyed beauty felt trapped on the farm which she had hardly left since she was born. She began to show attitude towards her younger brother Tommy and she was frustrated from working all day on the farm, mostly alone on various types of machinery that she was an expert in driving and maintaining.

She saw on the television that there was a dance at the Golden Town community hall and she decided, "I'm 18 years old, I have a driver's licence, and I'm going to that dance on my own!'

One day after she finished work, she went into her little brother Tommy's bedroom, swore at him and called him a bludger. Tommy shrugged and without saying a word continued playing on his trusty computer.

Caroline stood there fuming, hands on her hips, staring at him. He turned around in his swivel chair and smiled at her, saying, "There's a chair over there if you want to watch me play."

Slamming the door behind her, she stormed into the kitchen. Her mother was making tea and asked, "What's wrong, Caroline?"

"I'm sick of this! I work my guts out every day in the heat and flies while that brat in there just plays games in a nice cool bedroom all day and night!"

"Don't you ever call your brother a brat again! Is that understood?"

"Yes, mum, but it's not fair!"

Her mother gave her a look and she knew only too well not to continue the conversation. She changed tack and said, "In two Saturday's time, there's a dance in Golden Town that I've decided to go to."

"Have you asked your father?"

"No, And I don't have to. I'm 18."

"Maybe so, but its advisable," Caroline smiled at her mum, left the kitchen, and found her father sitting at the dining room table with a pile of bills he was going through. "Mum said I should let you know that I'm going to the Golden Town dance Saturday week."

He looked up at his daughter, who had the determined look on her face that he had loved since she was a toddler.

"Who's taking you?" he asked.

"I'm going on my own."

He smiled at her saying, "You're not going on your own, Caroline. In the past when you were much younger, we went as a family and it was safer then."

"Yes, I remember. But Dad, I'm 18 and I want to go on my own. And you can't stop me!"

"Caroline, I'm very well aware of how old you are and what a beautiful woman you've become. That's the reason I think you should go with someone for your protection."

Just when it looked like getting heated between father and daughter, her mother walked in saying,

"I was listening to the conversation, and I agree with both of you. So I have a suggestion. I haven't been to a dance for years, and its about time I went to one, don't you think, John?"

Not quite knowing how to answer his wife, he blurted out, "Okay, I'll take you."

The Saturday of the dance arrived. Caroline was getting nervous about going and said to her mother, "Mum, I've changed my mind, I've decided not to go as I haven't got anything to wear." And she burst into tears.

Her mother had anticipated this and had secretly been working hard sewing a dress for her daughter from a pattern, using some bright yellow material she'd bought years ago and never used.

She went into her bedroom and brought out the dress saying, "Try this one."

Her daughter looked at the beautiful yellow dress and started crying again.

"Don't get tears on this," she scolded, handing the dress to her daughter.

"Go and try it on and show your father."

Excitedly Caroline ran to her bedroom and tried the dress on in front of her mirror. When she heard her mother knock on the door, she said, "Come in, Mum. This dress is beautiful. Thank you!"

"You'll need this as well," her mother said, handing her a makeup kit. "Sit down and I'll help you do your face, then you can help me with mine."

She left and came back a few minutes later with the navy blue dress she was wearing to the dance and a set of pearl earring and necklace.

"I bought them years ago but have never worn them, so they're yours now. I should have given them to you years ago. But we've all been working so hard on the farm for the past few years, seven days a week, we've had no need to dress up."

Caroline put them on straight away, then looked at her mother and gave her a hug saying, "Thank you! They're beautiful."

They spent some time in front of Caroline's mirror, and came out into the kitchen hand in hand, to three gawking males.

"What do you think, Dad?"

He looked at his daughter and then his wife saying, "I'm not sure who'll be the Belle of the Ball, but I'm looking at one of the winners right here, for sure."

Caroline laughed at her two brothers, who were both still looking at their sister in amazement.

They arrived at the dance, leaving Tommy behind who didn't want to go to any silly dance.

Michael and Craig decided that they would go, Michael to try to pick up a girl, while Craig was not at all interested in girls.

While her other three, Michael, Caroline and Tommy, were outspoken, Craig, who was his mother's favourite, was quite the opposite. He was timid and quite skinny and short unlike his older brother and sister, who were both taller than he was. He also had to put up with Tommy, measuring himself up against him, saying, "I'm almost as tall as you already."

Secretly he was studying the Holy Bible and always had one in the harvester. His mother suspected his intentions but never approached him about it. Everyone in the family knew he read the Bible a lot but they had grown used to it over the years and paid little attention to it.

When they walked into the Golden Town community hall, all eyes were on Caroline who looked quite stunning in her bright yellow dress, which accentuated her long flowing blonde hair and pearl necklace and earrings. Her deep blue eyes were catching the fluorescent lighting and were shining brightly with excitement.

There was a rush from the boys to dance with her. Caroline limited them to one dance each until Jack, the owner's son from the adjoining farm, danced with her. Jack could not take his eyes off her. From time to time, their eyes met which made Caroline blush.

To Caroline's surprise, Jack would not let any other boys dance with her. She didn't mind, as she wanted to dance with Jack anyway as she had a long time crush on him,

Jack was a tall, lanky 18 year old, who was slightly built and looked more like an accountant than a farmer, with dark hair and a pale complexion from spending all day on his computer like his mainly online friend, Caroline's brother Tommy.

Both farms were about the same size and concentrated on wheat farming and sheep. But unlike Caroline's family, Jack's parents were wealthy and hired workers to look after the farm and harvest the wheat, while Caroline's family did everything.

Susanne squeezed her husband's hand, looked into his eyes, and said to him watching Jack and Caroline, "I think we've déjà vu happening right before our eyes, John. Do you remember when you wouldn't let any boy dance with me?"

Nodding at Jack fending off would-be suiters and Caroline not complaining about it, "Look," she said. "That was you, and I remember when I first rocked up at Golden Town looking for gold and emeralds and I found a diamond instead."

"Maybe so, but that's my daughter and he's not me!"

Nodding towards their daughter holding onto Jack and dancing close, Susanne said, "You're a brave man, John, but maybe not that courageous."

Not knowing what to say, he said nothing.

The night was at its end, except for the choice of the Belle of the Ball. Some of the ladies were standing on the stage. Caroline's mother grabbed her hand and led her to the stage.

One after the other the contestants moved forward when their names were called and each received generous praise. When Caroline moved forward, the noise of the applause was deafening. Blushing, she received a bunch of daffodils that matched her dress. All of the other contestants left the stage clapping Caroline.

Then Jack jumped on the stage and grabbed her hand and said, "Come on, let's get out of here." They ran out of the dance together, waving goodbye.

The following morning at 9 am, Jack walked Caroline to her door, and was about to kiss her goodbye when they were surprised to see her father coming out of the farmhouse front door. He said "So where do you think you've been, Caroline?"

"Why?" Caroline challenged her father.

"Your mother and I were worried about you. I was giving you another half hour and was then going to drive over to your place," he replied, looking at Jack,

"Where have you two been all night?"

"Dad, I'm not a baby anymore. I'm 18 years old. And yesterday you were worried about who was going to protect me going to the dance."

Before he could reply, his wife called out from the kitchen, "I've made a cup of tea for the five of us. Tommy is joining us, if you have time Jack, as he wants to say hi to you."

They walked inside and sat down. Knowing her father was still expecting an explanation, Caroline opened the conversation.

"Dad, Jack was a proper gentleman all night, if that's what you're wondering about, and I felt very safe with him. We decided to chat all night on the banks of the creek that both our farms share and watch the sunrise. We stayed in Jack's car as I didn't want to ruin my beautiful new dress."

Her father was about to say something when his wife said, "I bet it was a beautiful sunrise."

"The most beautiful sunrise I've ever seen, Mum," Tommy replied, trying to change the subject for his sister,

"Jack, I'm sorry for thrashing you last week on your new computer game, mate."

"No, you're not," replied Jack, smiling.

"You're right; I thoroughly enjoyed it," Tommy said laughing.

From that day onwards, Jack spent a lot of time with Caroline at the Willis farm. If he wasn't with Caroline, he was playing computer games most days in Tommy's bedroom.

This was starting to annoy John Willis and his wife because it was beginning to affect the running of the farm. Caroline used to spend much more time working on the farm but now was cutting her days short to be with Jack. And they knew that as long as Jack was playing computer games with Tommy, there was no chance at all of him ever working on the farm like his brothers and sister.

They both wanted to say something, but did not want to upset Caroline. She noticed this and decided to say something to Jack about it.

"Jack, I like you, but my parents and I think that you're spending too much time here and we're not as rich as your parents who can afford to hire workers."

Jack looked at Caroline, who had a tear in her eye. He walked up to her and kissed her cheek and left, spinning his back wheels all the way to the Willis entrance gate.

Caroline started to worry when after two weeks, she still had not seen or heard from Jack and was missing him. She asked Tommy if he had heard from him but he said he hadn't, which wasn't exactly right as they played computer games against one another most days and nights.

"I haven't heard from him, Sis, but he's on here at the moment, taking a beating as usual on his new computer game."

"Show me."

"Can I take your place for a while, Tommy?"

"Why not?" And he rolled his chair to one side as Caroline took over the controls of his computer. Not knowing what she was doing, Jack all of a sudden was winning easily,

"Is that still you, Tommy?"

"No, it's me, Caroline. Why haven't you dropped in to see me?"

"I didn't think you wanted to see me, Caroline."

"Of course I do, but not every day. It interferes too much with the running of the farm."

"That's a relief! I'm on my way; I'll pick you up in half an hour."

Jack missed Caroline so much that he decided to do something about strengthening their relationship. He picked her up and said, "What time does the Golden Town's jewellers close, Caroline?

"Why?"

"I thought we should get engaged."

CHAPTER 6

"You're a fine one! You don't even bother to see or talk to me for weeks, and then you ask me to get engaged to you." Smiling at him,

"The jeweller is closed, but I'll give you one of my rings so you can buy me an engagement ring the correct size, which is size seven."

"So that means yes?"

"Of course I'll marry you, silly. I love you."

The following day Caroline was up bright and early and drove an old ring over to Jack at his farm.

That afternoon Jack drove to the Willis farm, counting the five spokes on the farm's entrance wheel. He wondered if Tommy's spoke would ever be fitted to the wheel but he doubted it as he knew Tommy was adamant that was never going to happen.

He had parked his car next to a massive harvester that one of Caroline's brothers would have driven all day when he saw Caroline's father walking towards the house. He offered him a lift and nervously said, "John, I need to talk to you."

Farmer John Willis was feeling exhausted and said, "Thanks for the lift. I'm too tired to talk now, mate. Some other time maybe?"

He got out of the car and left Jack sitting there, stunned.

Caroline saw Jack's car and got down from her harvester. She had started to run towards the farmhouse when she saw his car disappear into the distance at speed.

When she arrived at the farmhouse, she ran in the door and demanded to know why Jack drove off as he did.

"I don't know Caroline.He said he wanted to talk to me but I told him that I was too tired to chat."

"Dad! You can be such a bastard some times! Do you know what he was going to talk to you about?"

"What's wrong, Caroline?" asked her mother.

"Did you notice that I left early this morning and started harvesting as soon as I got back?"

"Yes, what's that got to do with Jack wanting to talk to your father?"

"This morning, I took a ring to Jack for measurement, as he was buying me an engagement ring today. And he was probably going to ask Dad if he could marry me."

"How was I supposed to know?" John Willis said to his wife, who was glaring at him. Then he brightened and said to her, "Come on, we haven't visited our neighbours for quite a while. Do you want to come too, Caroline?"

"No! Please don't go, Mum!"

"Ask Tommy if he wants to come if you don't."

Caroline opened Tommy's bedroom door and, pointing to her mother and father, said, "Those two want to know if you want to go with them to Jack's house."

Her mother walked up to her saying, "Caroline! Don't speak like that! Your father was tired and had no idea what Jack was going to ask him. I think you should come with us as well."

Tommy said, "Thanks, but I think I'll stay here and thrash your boyfriend on his new computer game."

Caroline poked her tongue out at her brother, closed the door and said, "I will come, but I'll stay in the car."

When they arrived, Jack's parents came out to greet them. They shook hands and were invited inside out of the heat.

"Where's Jack?" asked John Willis.

"In his bedroom," answered his mother. "I'll get him. Tea or coffee?"

Jack came out of his bedroom. Before he could say anything, John Willis said to him, "I believe you were going to ask me something earlier."

"I was, but I've changed my mind. I don't think I could live with Caroline, she's too much like you!"

Jack walked out the front door, leaving his and Caroline' parents stunned, only to find Caroline kicking the tyres of her father's car. Jack walked up behind her, kissed her on her neck, and said, "So what's that wheel done to deserve that treatment?"

Caroline turned to see Jack standing behind her, smiling.

"My dad is upset with himself that he didn't listen to you earlier."

"Was he?"

"Yes, he said so driving here."

"That changes everything, Caroline. Come on; I'll ask for your hand in marriage now."

They walked into Jack's large house that had recently been refurbished. Caroline was wondering why perfectly good furniture was stacked in a shed as they walked past it arm in arm.

Jack noticed Caroline looking at it and said to her, "Mum replaces all our furniture every five years and sends it to charity."

Caroline smiled and said, "That furniture's better than the furniture we have in our house."

They walked in hand in hand smiling. Realising he didn't have the engagement ring on him, Jack raced to his bedroom and came back with the ring box in his hand.

He walked up to John Willis and said, "Mr Willis, Caroline and I love each other very much, and I'm asking you for her hand in marriage."

John Willis smiled at his daughter, his wife and Jack's parents and said to Jack, shaking his hand, "Is that an engagement ring you're holding?"

"Yes."

Jack immediately walked over to Caroline, who was blushing, and dropping to one knee, he said, "Will you marry me, Caroline?"

"Yes, of course I will, on one condition. After our honeymoon we return here because I'm not just the daughter of John Willis, I'm also a spoke in the Willis Family Wheel."

All the parents clapped as Jack placed the engagement ring on Caroline's finger.

She looked at it smiling. "It's beautiful! And it fits perfectly."

Jack's father had greying hair and was slightly built. He always wore a suit, no matter how hot he was. He opened a bottle of his finest champagne and toasted his son and his fiancé on their engagement.

"It'll have to be a three-bedroom house with bedrooms for our future grandchildren," he replied.

This got the whole group laughing, except for Caroline, who replied to Jack's father seriously, "So who mentioned children?"

Jack's father looked at his wife, who was always well dressed and much younger, with shining emerald eyes and jet black hair. Then at Caroline's parents and then at Jack, who laughed at his father saying, "Dad, you've just been had.

"Don't worry, Caroline and I have often talked about what our children will look like."

Caroline gave him a kiss on the cheek smiling, and said,

" A three-bedroom house is so very generous. And you're right. Hopefully we'll have a boy and a girl, soon after we're married. I was just kidding."

Jack and Caroline looked at quite a few homes and finally decided on one and excitedly showed Jack's parents. They studied the plans and were impressed.

Jack's father said, "Thanks. I'll get the ball rolling and will let you know the completion date so you can plan your wedding around its completion."

CHAPTER 7

After some time, Caroline began to have second thoughts about marrying Jack as she became unsure he would be capable of putting bread on the table for her and her future family. He never did anything, he never helped on his parent's farm, but he played computer games all the time.

One day she decided to broach the subject. She finished work early but had to wait for Jack, who came out from Tommy's room half an hour later.

"Jack, we need to talk!"

"What's up?"

"Its only fair to tell you, before your father goes any further with his wedding present, that I've changed my mind about marrying you."

"Why? I love you, and I know you love me."

"Jack, I'm so sorry," she said, handing him her engagement ring.

Jack looked at the ring saying, "Why?"

"I've decided that if I'm going to marry anyone, it will be to a man and not a boy."

"What do you mean, Caroline?"

"Jack, if and when I marry someone, that person will have to show me that he's capable of working for a living and will be able to support a family. Sadly, Jack, I do love you, but you're not a man, but a child."

Jack replied, "Don't worry, Caroline. When my mother and father pass, I'll have more money than you can point a stick at."

And he handed the engagement ring back to her, kissed her on the cheek and left, leaving Caroline flabbergasted.

Jack drove home, not at all worried about what Caroline had said to him, as he knew he was a man, and there wasn't any need for him to work ever.

Late one afternoon, Jack's father dropped into the Willis farm with news for his son and Caroline,

Susanne Willis welcomed him in and told Jack his father was in the kitchen and wanted to speak to him and Caroline when she finishes work.

Then she said to Jack's father, "Caroline, her father and brothers will be here in half an hour. Its not quite sunset, and they rarely finish work until then. Except some times when Caroline stops early to see Jack. But she often gets upset when she finishes work early to see him but he still plays games in Tommy's room. She doesn't say anything, but has an angry look that her brothers know only too well. But Jack doesn't appear even to notice it."

"Mrs Willis."

"You can call me Susanne."

"I can hear them coming. I'll put a pot of tea on for Caroline and Craig, and some beers for John and Michael, Maybe you'd like a beer with them?"

"A glass of wine would be nice."

"Wine? We only drink that on special occasions, which I suppose this is, but sorry, we don't have any in the house."

"Tea will do then."

She handed him his cup as Michael, Caroline, Craig and John Willis walked in and sat down, after shaking hands. Caroline received a kiss on her cheek from Jack's father.

"I'll let Jack and Tommy know you are here again," Caroline said to her mother.

"We know what they're doing, Mum! Playing stupid computer games while we slave our guts out!"

About 15 minutes later, Jack and Tommy appear from the bedroom. Jack shook hands with everyone and went to kiss Caroline but she turned her head away.

"What's the matter, Caroline?" asked Jack.

"I told you yesterday, but you chose not to listen to a bloody word I said!"

Susanne smiled saying, "Jack's father has some good news for Jack and Caroline.

Jack's father stood up and said,

"I have some good news. The Local Council has approved the plans for your house and I have contacted the builders. The proposed completion date is exactly six months to the day. I have a written contract stating if the builder goes over this time, he'll be fined $5000 per week. So you can guarantee it will be finished on time. You'll have to allow another month for carpet, furniture, kitchens, bathrooms and curtains etc. to be fitted."

Caroline stood up and said to Jack's father, "Thank you for your kind offer of a three-bedroom house for our wedding present. It's very generous but I've changed my mind about marrying Jack."

Jack jumped up and asked, "What are you talking about Caroline?"

"You didn't hear a word that I said to you yesterday, did you?"

"What, that nonsense about me not being man enough to support you and a family? I told you there's no need to work to support you. When mum and dad pass, I'll inherit their fortune."

Jack's father stood up and said, "Caroline, I can't blame you one bit. It appears my wife and I have made a great mistake letting Jack have a free pass on everything. And believe me, this will stop from this moment on!

"Jack, there'll be no more free pass for you. From this moment on you'll have to find a paying job or you'll be working on our farm from sunrise to sunset, like Caroline and her family do. And then, and only then, will I give the builders the go-ahead to build the house!

"And furthermore, I may not decide to leave everything I own to you. I may decide you're not worthy and sign it all over to charity once your mother passes away.

"And it pains me to say this, son, but as it stands at the moment, I agree with Caroline! Its mine and your mother's fault, and not yours, but if you want to marry Caroline, you'll have to prove you're worthy. At the moment, it's obvious you're not up to Caroline's standard of a husband."

Jack said, "Okay! As from tomorrow, Caroline, I will work from sunrise to sunset to prove to you that I'm man enough to provide for a family."

The following morning Jack's father took Jack to his foreman saying,

"Jack's decided he wants to be a worker on the farm and wants to learn everything there is to know about wheat and sheep. He wants to work as hard as all the other hands we have on the farm. I want a weekly report from you."

The foreman looked Jack up and down saying, "He'll toughen up in time.

"Come on, you can be my offsider, which doesn't mean you're a foreman's assistant, but a worker, carrying out all kinds of jobs, and some will be extremely dirty and others will be back-breaking."

Jack looked at his father and nodded in agreement. Then Jack followed the foreman who was wondering just what had caused all this. However, he thought he could always do with an extra pair of hands.

Jack surprised the foreman as although he was extremely muscle sore, he kept going, only stopping for breaks with the other farmworkers who took him under their wing and showed him everything they knew.

At first, he was too tired and sore even to drive his car to see Caroline which worried her. She often asked Tommy if he had been playing computer games with him. The answer was always no.

After a few weeks Caroline decided to drive over to see him after work but found him fast asleep and did not wake him. She noticed how sunburnt he was.

His mother told Jack the following afternoon after work, "Caroline has been to see you, but she decided not to wake you."

Despite hardly able to stand up from his aching muscles, Jack walked to the car and drove over to the Willis farm. Caroline heard his car coming and ran outside to greet him.

"How's it going, my future husband? You look exhausted. Can I get you a glass of milk or water?"

"A beer thanks!"

Caroline thought to herself, 'A beer, not his normal water or milk. Wow! In only two weeks what a change."

CHAPTER 8

Michael, Caroline and Craig were always complaining to their mother and father that it wasn't fair that they had to work hard on the farm all day, putting up with the dirt, heat and flies, while their brother Tommy stayed at home in the fresh farmhouse and played computer games all day and night.

One sweltering summer day, the three older children rebelled. Instead of joining their hard-working father working the farm, they all decided to stay at home like Tommy. They played games on their computers too, which left their father having to do all the work on his own and getting exhausted.

Susanne could not help as she was busy teaching Tommy 'School of the Air' as the promised governess had still not arrived, due to the shortage of suitable school teachers.

Their father did the best he could, working as hard as he could. Even after sunset, he would still be working, while the other family members played computer games.

Unfortunately, they did not get enough seeds planted and with persistent drought, the crop was not enough to feed the family or pay their bills, including the power bill. As they did not have enough money to pay the electricity bill, power to the farm was disconnected.

The three brothers and sister had gone their whole lives expecting electricity would be there for them with a flick of a switch. They had a great surprise when nothing in the farmhouse worked. They ran to the television, the video, the electric jug, toaster and even their computers but they all refused to light up. Also the light switch did not turn the lights on.

They looked at one another in disbelief and did not know what to do. Caroline looked out of the window and saw her usually strong father hunched over in tears with his wife trying to comfort him. When Caroline got there, he was actually sobbing, and she hugged her father and also started crying when she saw the tears even welling up in her mother's eyes.

The Willis farm continued to be in drought with no rain expected, causing Mr Willis to get depressed. His youngest son Tommy was looking for work at nearby Emerald, as was his sister Caroline at Golden Town.

Caroline managed to get a job at the local hotel for four hours each night, after working on the farm from sunrise to sunset, to try to earn some money to get the power back on.

With her feisty nature and good looks the publican was drawing in a lot of new faces. One of the conditions of her employment was that she would have ten free beers for her brothers and father. Every day Michael, after a hard day's work, liked to go to the local pub for a few free beers, thanks to his sister Caroline. His brother Craig at times joined him, as well as their father.

CHAPTER 9

One day a colossal shearer strolled into the hotel bar. He was thirsty as anything, pushed Craig out of the way and slammed his fist on the bar, shouting at Caroline who was drying glasses behind the bar. "I want a beer now!"

Michael said to him, "Who do you think you are? My brother was before you! Wait your turn."

Craig interjected saying, "Its okay, Michael. I'm not as thirsty as this guy," pointing his finger at the shearer.

"Who do you think you're pointing the finger at?"

Caroline interjected and said to the shearer, "I don't know what your issue is, but Craig was before you, and I'm serving him first."

"Do you want the usual Craig?"

"Yes, please, but you can serve him first."

"No! You were first. The usual, Craig?" she asked, glaring at him

"Yes, please."

Michael was watching the huge thirsty shearer, who grabbed Craig's arm and spun him around so they were facing one another, with the shearer towering over Craig as he prepared to punch him in the face.

Michael grabbed the shearer's right arm, forcing his fist to miss Craig's face. It was unfortunate for the huge shearer that he had met his match with Michael, who landed three punches on his chin, knocking him out.

Just then his father walked in saying, "What happened here?"

Caroline said to him smiling, "This thing," pointing to the shearer laying on the floor out cold, "came storming up to the bar, pushing Craig out of the way, demanding to be served first. When I refused, he swung Craig around and Michael grabbed his arm just enough to make him miss punching Craig's face.

"Michael then showed this thug that pushing around a Golden Town farmer isn't as easy as pushing helpless sheep around while they are being shorn."

The shearer started to stir and came to. Standing over him John Willis said to him, "Drink this beer, and then I'd get back in your pickup truck, and in future, if you come in for a beer, show more respect for the people in front of you."

The shearer looked at the tall farmer who was handing him a beer that Caroline had just passed to her father. He was still groggy, holding his chin, wondering if it was broken. He drank the glass of beer straight down and departed, to a massive roar of laughter from everyone in the bar.

Caroline said, "That'll teach that shearer not to pick on Golden Town farmers."

Craig said to his big brother, "Thanks, Michael, but I could have taken him."

"Of course you would have, Craig," said Michael, putting his arm around him and leading him to a table where they sat down to enjoy their beers with their father.

The shearer came back to the hotel bar's door, looked in and decided not to go in. He went back to his pick up truck and sat there fuming for a while, listening to country music and the air conditioning which had a calming effect on him.

Half an hour later, he walked into the hotel, walked up to Caroline and said, "Can I please have another beer?"

Caroline, who was still fuming over the way he treated her brother, said to him, "Not until you apologise to Craig Willis over there!"

"Are they the Willis' from the Willis farm?"

"Yes, why?" asked Caroline.

"I've heard they have a flock of sheep that need shearing."

"That's the man to see, over there. His name is John Willis, my father."

"I can't see any resemblance."

'I take after my mother. And unless you apologise to my brother Craig, you'll never have another beer served to you as long as I work here ever again! And that's every night."

Smiling at Caroline, he strolled over to the Willis table. As he did Michael jumped up, ready for round two of the fight.

His father summed up the situation quickly and pulled Michael down by his shirt that was hanging over his belt. "How can we help you? I believe you owe my son Craig here an apology."

The shearer looked at Craig and said, "Your sister over there said if I don't apologise to her brother, I'll never drink in here again."

They all looked over to Caroline and started laughing,

"So I'd best give you my best apology, Craig. Sorry mate!"

Craig stood up and offered his hand in friendship.

The shearer said to him, "Thirst got the better of me!"

"Sit down," said John Willis,

"What I came back to the pub for was another beer, and I'm out of work and hungry and in desperate need of some kind of work. A guy I spoke to earlier said he thought you had a flock of sheep, ready for shearing."

"True, but did he also tell you that we're broke?"

"Yes, he did. But I thought that if you give me food and lodging, we would both be happy."

"I hope you don't mind eating mutton every night, and have you got an alcohol problem, mate?" asked John Willis,

'Nup! I was just as thirsty as a lizard drinking."

"Well, sit down. You've already met Michael, I believe?" He touched his chin smiling,

"Too bloody right, I have."

Caroline, who was listening to the conversation, arrived at the table with four beers, saying, "On the house!"

Caroline was finishing her shift when her replacement Sheila walked in. At once, her eyes turned to the giant shearer sitting at the Willis's table.

She whispered in Caroline's ear, "Who's that good looking guy sitting with your family?"

"Good looking he may be but, in my opinion, he's just a brute with a glass jaw."

Sheila was tall and skinny with dark hair and piercings through her tongue, with far too many tattoos for the likings of Caroline's brothers.

"He's a shearer out of work, who tried to bully Craig and Michael knocked him out."

Still whispering. Caroline handed the bar over to Sheila and sat down to have a beer with her family.

It wasn't long before Sheila came to the table and pulled a chair up, placing it next to the shearer,

"G'day mate, I'm Sheila, you?

"Is that your real name Sheila?"

"Nup. That's what I like to be called."

"What's your name?"

"Well Sheila, if you're not going to tell me your real name, you can call me The Shearer. Or just plain Shearer if you like."

The Willis's all burst out laughing at the same time.

Sheila asked about what happened earlier, "Oh nothing, just a friendly get together between two hotheads." The subject was dropped.

As Sheila asked if anyone else needed drinks, she said, "Well shearer, I finish at midnight, if you want to walk me home."

From that moment on they were inseparable. The minute he finished work, he was knocking on her door.

It wasn't long before all the sheep on the Willis farm were shorn and he moved out of the bunkhouse and moved in with Sheila. Later he got a job as a jack-of-all-trades at the pub and elsewhere.

In time Michael and the shearer ended up good mates. He often used to grab his jaw saying, "I'm sure it's broken!"

CHAPTER 10

onths before the power to the farm was shut off, Tommy had come under pressure as he was getting close to leaving school. It was a long family tradition that as soon as a child was old enough to leave school, he or she was expected to start work on the Willis family farm.

Tommy did not know how he was going to get around this and asked some friends on his computer if they knew where he could find a job when he left school.

One Saturday, one of his friends he only knew from communicating on his computer months earlier, rode up to his house and knocked. His mother was quite surprised to see a young lady in jodhpurs and a riding helmet at the door asking for Tommy.

Tommy's mother took her inside and said to her, "You're Kathy from School of the Air. I recognise your voice."

"Yes," she replied, smiling sweetly at Mrs Willis, who now realised why Tommy was now interested in School of the Air.

She took her to the bedroom and called out, "Tommy, you have a visitor." She pointed to Tommy's closed door then left.

Tommy heard his mother say he had a visitor. Thinking it was Jack he called back, "Thanks, mum, come in Jack."

Tommy looked up and to his great surprise saw a young lady standing at his door holding her riding hat, smiling at him,

"Hi, I'm Kathy. We were talking on the computer about you looking for work a few months ago."

"Yes," stammered Tommy who wasn't used to talking to girls, especially this very pretty one. He was blushing, feeling very uncomfortable, until she said, "So this is your I Mac 27 computer. Very impressive!"

"When we had the power on it was."

"Sit down," said Tommy, who could hardly keep his voice from giving away his excitement at getting a visit from Kathy who lived on a nearby farm.

Soon the conversation changed to Kathy asking Tommy if he was genuine about looking for work in a few weeks when he left school.

"Yes, Kathy, I'm looking for work. Why?"

"I heard the Green Gem Stud Farm at Emerald is looking for a good stable hand."

Tommy laughed at her, saying, "Kathy, thank you, but I don't know anything at all about horses, particularly racehorses. As a matter of fact, the circus merry go round is as close as I've ever come to a horse. I spend all my time here on my computer."

"Come outside and I'll introduce you to Tex, my horse."

Tommy's mother watched through the window as Kathy took Tommy outside to see her horse. She said, "Tex, meet Tommy."

Laughing, she said, "I'll show you how to put a harness on."

Tommy did this quite well, much to his mother's surprise.

"See, it's quite easy. You'll soon learn, and the guys on the stud farm will help and show you. I know one of them who'll look after you for me. Just tell them that you've been strapping at the Doomben race track.

"One thing I'd best let you know is that some racehorses bite and if they do, they have soft noses and punch them on the nose to show them you're the boss."

Armed with all these lies, Tommy, who looked older than he was, left the Willis family farm.

The Stud Farm's foreman was soon interviewing him. When their huge 17.2 hand stallion named Savage All leant over the rail and went to bite, Tommy, with quick reflex, punched the horse on the nose and it galloped away.

The manager said to Tommy, "So when do you want to start? We have accommodation in the bunkhouse if you like."

"How about today?" replied Tommy.

"Come on, I'll introduce you to the guys."

Tommy was introduced to the other workers and shown the horses that would be his responsibility. They included the breeding stallion Savage All, another stallion, and six of Queensland's top racehorses that were spelling at the stud farm before returning to training and racing in Brisbane and Sydney. Tommy did not know what to do as they approached the bunkhouse but Kathy's friend Phil came out saying, "Don't worry, Tommy. Kathy has asked me to look after you and show you what to do here."

The foreman left Tommy with Phil and left.

"Thanks, Phil, I didn't realise I'd be working with the horses. I thought I'd be painting fences and things like that."

Apart from one incident when Tommy managed to escape through a window when Savage All trapped him in his stable as he took his feed bins in, everything went very well.

One of Tommy's horses won the Sydney Cup and the Tancred Cup and the owner handed Tommy a roll of notes for doing such a great job strapping his horse Gallant that was back at the stud farm for a spell.

Tommy loved the job, and the horses liked him. One of them that he nicknamed Nuisance loved to take his hat off his head and prance away with it, with his head held high. He usually dropped it on the ground and stomped in it. And soon as Tommy went to retrieve it, Nuisance would pick it up with his teeth and run off with it neighing.

Tommy had been working on the stud farm for six months when one day the manager approached him, saying, "We've just drenched the mares in the back paddock. Can you keep an eye on them for me?"

Tommy, not knowing that drenching meant worming, asked the manager, "So where do I get the towels to dry them off?"

The manager gave Tommy a look of amazement. He could not believe what he had just heard and said, "What did you just say, Tommy?"

Tommy replied, "You said that you'd just drenched the mares in the back paddock. So I'm wondering where the towels are to dry them off."

"Tommy, please come with me."

They both walked up to the stud farm foreman. When the manager told the foreman what Tommy had said, he responded, "Tommy hasn't been honest with us. Pay him off immediately."

Tommy arrived back at home. The Willis family were all relieved when young Tommy shared the roll of money from Gallant's owner. It was not enough to get the power back on but helped feed his family and pay a few bills that his father was getting pressured about paying.

CHAPTER 11

One day, Craig saw the postman come through the gates to deliver some letters. He rode over to him and loaded them all onto his trike and, after thanking and saying goodbye to the postman, drove back to the house, forgetting the letters until much later when he remembered that they were in his back pocket of his overalls. He found everyone, except Tommy, in the kitchen sitting around the table. Craig put the letters down in front of his tired father, "It's from Brisbane, dad. It must be from Nan Mary!"

Their father quietly read the letter from his mother, not saying a word, shaking his head from side to side. Mrs Willis then read the letter and asked her husband if she could read it out loud to the children. He agreed and Susanne cleared her throat, looked at her children and moved a candle closer so she could read,

"Dear John and family, I have decided to come out to the farm and catch up with you all for a few weeks. I will be at the station at 1 pm on Monday if you can please pick me up."

Mr Willis dreaded the thought of his mother seeing the farm in the condition it was and not making any profit.

Mrs Willis went over to her husband and tried to comfort him, saying, "Your mother will understand."

He looked at the letter again and pushed the other letters away, got up and went for a walk on his own.

The children's grandmother, Mary, had spent her entire life on the Willis farm until her husband passed away and she decided it was too hard for her to look after the farm on her own.

When they got married all her children, except her eldest son John and his wife Susanne, wanted to leave the farm, as they had worked on it all their lives. John wanted to carry on the farm with his family.

His grandmother had thought this was a good idea. Now John did not want his mother to believe he had let the family down.

Mr Willis applied for a loan from the bank, which turned him down. Still, after he had paid all the shopkeepers with Tommy's money, he did manage to get some of the local shops to let him keep a tab until he had enough money to pay them back again.

He bought a small amount of food which was barely enough to feed the family, which was now basically living off the sheep on the farm.

The following Monday farmer John Willis put a few items on a tab from the local shops and picked up his mother from Golden Town railway station.

She was wearing a dark brown dress that made her look even older than she was. The years working and living on the farm in outback Queensland had taken its toll on the once beautiful Scottish lady who, when she arrived in Australia, had very soft white skin that was now all shrunk and wrinkled.

As old as she was, her son looked into her stunning, kind, light blue eyes that had never changed, smiled and kissed her on her forehead.

"Welcome," he said as he was picking up her bag.

As they climbed into the pickup truck, John's mother noticed the boxes of candles and five lamps and a drum of kerosene and a small number of groceries in the back but did not say a word.

As they drove through the farm gates, his mother noticed that what used to display a wagon wheel with five spokes now only had two spokes left, struggling to keep the outer rim in place.

When all his children refused to go on working on the farm, their father insisted they were no longer Willis spokes and removed them from the wagon wheel and placed them in the corner of the kitchen in plain sight, for his children to see. He hoped it would change their minds about not working, but to no avail.

John Willis noticed that she had seen this and realised she would have known why there were only two spokes left in the Willis family wheel.

But before he could say a word, she said, "I can't wait to get to the farmhouse and live under lamp and candlelight. It must be 20 years since your father and I went through the drought conditions you've recently found yourself in. If it makes you feel any better, your brother's farm at Rockhampton isn't faring well either from the drought.

"I imagine you've had your power shut off, having to use candles, lamps and kerosene with very little food in the truck."

The two months went by quickly, and the children's grandmother taught them a lot about surviving without power.

When she left, she looked at her grandchildren and said, "I've loved the past two months, and it has brought back great memories for me. The last time I was here, Tommy was in his room on his computer all the time and you other children were too involved in television and other things even to realise I was here."

She went on to say to them all, "You lucky children, I'm not sure if you realise but tomorrow is the start of the seeding season. I loved getting out with your late grandfather onto the farm.

"Actually, I did a lot of ploughing for the seed planting on the tractor, when we had earnt enough to buy one and a new plough. Before that, he used a horse to pull the plough and I used to go behind, dispersing the seed.

"After we purchased the tractor and plough things changed. I drove the tractor and he followed behind me, planting the seed from dawn to dusk, stopping only for meals.

"It pains me to say that if I weren't so old, I'd love to help your father with the seeding. I imagine you're all as excited about the seeding season as I used to be."

The matriarch grandmother, Mary, smiled at them all and gave everyone a hug and a kiss and also gave her son's wife Susanne a hug and a knowing look. She was helped into the car by her son and was soon waving goodbye.

When they arrived at Golden Town railway station, she gave her son an envelope full of money, saying, "I love you and your wife and children and want the Willis farm to continue, so please accept this and pay me back if you can."

Placing a finger to his lips, she handed him the money, which brought tears to both their eyes. When the train came, he helped her on. Mary hugged her son goodbye, wiping her eyes with a handkerchief, leaving them both in tears as the train pulled away.

Looking at the envelope and counting the money, he realised there was enough money to clear most of his debts and buy some food, but not enough to pay the electricity bill.

After a sleepless night, Michael said to his brothers and sister, "We need to talk now! Come with me!"

So the young people went into the shed that held a stack of hay, bags of seed, tractors, ploughs, graders and other farming equipment and Michael whispered, "We all know, except for Tommy, this is now the planting season and we all know what we should do."

Caroline, Craig and Michael read his mind and they each knew what Michael was thinking, as they looked at their youngest brother Tommy.

Michael continued looking at Tommy and said to him, "Tommy, we're going out onto the farm to start ploughing in preparation for seed planting. Will you help us, or are you going to sit in the dark house all day looking at a blank computer screen?"

Tommy looked up at Michael, then to Caroline, who had pleading eyes, then to Craig and Michael, then said, "Look, guys, I'd love to help, but honestly, I don't know how to."

Craig put his arm around his younger brother and said, "Come with me every day and I'll teach you everything I know."

Tommy smiled at his brothers and sister and said, "Well spoken, brother. It looks like I'm going to be a spoke in the Willis family wheel after all."

The first thing after their secret meeting, they each collected their spoke from the kitchen and then went to the farm gate with a ladder. And in turn they each replaced the spoke that their father had removed, including Tommy's, on to the wagon wheel. Tommy brought his from the back of his wardrobe where he had put it after his father had given it to him when he finished School of the Air.

That day their father and mother were surprised to see all their children, including the youngest Tommy, ploughing the adjoining paddock. At lunchtime when they stopped what they were doing, they rode over to talk to them. On the way, Mrs Willis told her husband not to make a big deal out of Tommy working.

When they got there, their father said, "Wow! Look how much you've ploughed. Great work! I'm proud of you all! Come on, let's all go to the farmhouse and get something to eat."

"Why don't you come with us to look at the wheel on the gate, Mum and Dad," said Michael, and the entire family, including Tommy, drove out to the family farm gate.

"Look," said Tommy, proudly pointing to all the spokes in the Willis family wheel above the gate which included his shiny new spoke.

As soon as the Willis family finished planting all their seed, the rains came, producing a vital crop which made them a lot of money.

This money allowed the family to get their electricity back on, to stock the now full shed and pay all their bills.

When it was seed planting time again, Tommy was the first onto a tractor and before he started the engine, shouted aloud to his father so that everyone could hear, "Come on, father, from one spoke to another. Let's get these Willis family tractor wheels rolling."

Later after the harvesting had finished on both farms, Caroline and Jack walked up to Jack's father and mother hand in hand.

Caroline said, "Dad, I think you can start the construction on Jack's and my family home."

She was smiling at Jack who was now fully fit and educated in all things farming, and she was now once again proudly wearing her engagement ring.

The wedding was a typical country one, with everyone, including children, attending the Golden Town church, and the wedding reception at Jack's farm.

During the speeches, Jack's father tearfully expressed what a man Carolyn had turned his son into in a short time.

John Willis walked over to where Tommy was sitting, pulled him up out of his chair and put his arm around him. saying, "And this spoke has surprised us all," which brought a lot of laughter from the wedding guests.

THE END

ABOUT THE AUTHOR

David F R Perry has been writing since 1997 and has published a number of books.

Recently he has been concentrating mainly on children's books.

His fantastic character Hippity Hoppity the White Kangaroo features in six of them, with another just finished.

Other books David has recently published are: The Tell Tale Bird, The Holiday Adventures of Bonza and Sonja The Humpback Whales. A science fiction novel entitled The 8th Re-Creation Of Man, and his amazing story 'The Secret Ship That Saves The World.

He lives in the Blue Mountains, west of Sydney, Australia.

He helmed his racing yacht offshore winning several championships. Although now retired, he is still a member of The Royal Motor Yacht Club.

David is also a member of the New South Wales Art Gallery, and various writing groups. David has certificates from TAFE and the University of NSW for Creative Writing, Writing Simple Stories, Writing Extended Stories, and Editing Text.

9 781638 121190